Transportation

Paul Dowswell

Heinemann Library
Chicago, Illinois

Customer Service 888-454-2279

Visit our website at www.heinemannlibrary.com

06 05 04 03 02
10 9 8 7 6 5 4 3 2 1

Designed by Tinstar Design
Illustrations by Nicholas Beresford-Davies & Martin Griffin
Originated by Ambassador Litho
Printed in Hong Kong/China

Library of Congress Cataloging-in-Publication Data
Dowswell, Paul.
    Transportation / Paul Dowswell.
      p. cm. -- (Great inventions)
    Includes bibliographical references and index.
    ISBN 1-58810-216-5 (library binding)
    1. Transportation--History--Juvenile literature. 2.
  Inventions--Juvenile literature. [1. Transportation. 2. Inventions.] I.
  Title. II. Series.
  HE152 .D68 2001
  388'.09--dc21

                  00-012412

Acknowledgments
The Publishers would like to thank the following for permission to reproduce photographs:
Corbis, pp. 4, 5, 6, 14, 15, 28, 35, 37, 41; Hulton Getty, pp. 9, 11; AKG/Erich Lessing, p. 10; Science and Society, pp. 12, 18, 19, 22, 24; Mary Evans Picture Library, pp. 13, 23, 26; AKG, p. 20, 31, 38; R. N. Submarine Museum, p. 16; Empics Ltd./Jon Buckle, p. 25; Culture Archive, p. 27; Motoring Picture Library, p. 29; Science Photo Library/U.S. Library of Congress, p. 33; Aviation Picture Library/Austin J. Brown, p. 36; Science Photo Library/David Parker, p. 40; Aviation Images, p. 42; Science Photo Library/Jim Amos, p. 43.

Cover photographs: Empics (left), Photodisc (top right), Corbis (bottom right)

Some words are shown in bold, **like this.** You can find out what they mean by looking in the glossary.

A note about dates: in this book, dates are followed by the letters B.C.E. (Before the Common Era) or C.E. (Common Era). This is instead of using the older abbreviations B.C. (Before Christ) and A.D. (*Anno Domini*, meaning "in the year of our Lord"). The date numbers are the same in both systems.

Contents

Introduction 4

Bridges, 10,000 B.C.E. 6

Roads, 4000 B.C.E. 8

Wheel, 3500 B.C.E. 10

Sailing Ship, 3100 B.C.E. 12

Horse Travel, 2000 B.C.E. 14

Submarine, 1620 C.E. 16

Steamship, 1783 18

Balloon, 1783 20

Steam Locomotive, 1804............................22

Bicycle, 1817..24

Subway, 1863..26

Motorcycle, 1885....................................28

Car, 1886 30

Airplane, 1903 32

Jet, 1930...34

Single-Rotor Helicopter, 1939......................36

Hovercraft, 1955....................................38

Supertanker, 1956..................................40

Jumbo Jet, 1969....................................42

Timeline...44

Glossary 46

More Books to Read 47

Index...48

Introduction

Getting from one place to another is an essential human activity. Without our ability to travel, human settlements would be cut off from each other. Some isolated parts of the world, such as Australia, New Zealand, and some Pacific islands, are populated by humans only because their distant ancestors used primitive boats to get there more than 50,000 years ago.

Primitive transportation

The first travelers used their feet to go everywhere. The dirt tracks and primitive bridges that marked popular routes are transportation's first inventions. Boats were developed long before land transportation, giving seaside and river communities a great advantage over other communities. From the earliest times, water was seen as the best way to transport heavy goods. This is still the case today. The biggest mobile objects ever made are enormous supertankers and **cargo** ships.

Animals were **domesticated** around 9000 B.C.E., and donkeys, camels, oxen, and horses were used to carry goods and people. The invention of the wheel in about 3500 B.C.E. was the most significant development in transportation for the next 5,000 years. Without it, animal-drawn wagons and chariots would not have been possible.

These camels are being used to carry people and goods across the Sahara Desert. Humans have been using animals as a form of transportation for at least 9,000 years.

4

Steam power

The first practical steam engine was invented in 1712, and it changed transportation forever. At sea, steam power freed sailors from their 5,000-year dependence on the wind and the tides. On land, steam-powered locomotives rapidly transformed the civilizations that used them, making possible long-distance transportation that was quick, cheap, and reliable. Britain had the first passenger railroad in the world in 1825. By 1850, 100 million passenger journeys were being made in Britain every year, and the rest of the world soon followed.

The Concorde can carry passengers from London to New York in three hours. Less than 60 years after the Wright brothers' first flight, in 1903, aircraft could fly at twice the speed of sound.

The engine as we know it

Another even more significant revolution arrived in 1885. Karl Benz produced the first gasoline-driven **internal combustion engine** and fitted it to a modified horse carriage. Today, barely a hundred years later, there are estimated to be 500 million cars in use. The internal combustion engine also allowed for the invention of other forms of transportation, including the airplane and helicopter. The jet engine, invented in 1930, completed a half-century of extraordinary developments in transportation **technology.** Today, passenger jets can travel from New York to London in just three hours, and **military** jets can fly a mile in less than three seconds.

Many inventions and discoveries happened independently of one another in several different countries. Others, such as the steam locomotive, combined many different ideas to make a distinct new form of transportation.

Bridges, 10,000 B.C.E.

The first bridges were probably just logs laid across narrow streams. However, when people began to **domesticate** animals, something wider was needed for them to cross. This led to the development of the first constructed bridges.

Pillars and beams

The pillar and beam bridge was made by building pillars at regular intervals, then laying beams across from one pillar to the next. The pillars were made of stone and the beams from stone slabs or timber. In the fourth century B.C.E., the Greek historian Herodotus described a pillar and beam bridge in what is now Iraq. It had 100 stone piers with timber beams and stretched over 660 feet (200 meters). Most early pillar and beam bridges had shorter spans.

Suspension bridges

A suspension bridge is a type of bridge in which the entire structure is suspended over a drop, and there are no piers. The first suspension bridges were made from vines that were tied to tree trunks on either side of a gorge or river bank. Such bridges were common in ancient India, China, and Africa, where they can still be seen today.

*This early pillar and beam bridge in Dartmoor, England, was probably built by the **Celts.** A new bridge has been built behind it.*

Pontoon bridges

Pontoon bridges work in the same way as pillar and beam bridges, except that boats are used as pillars. In Persia in what is now Iran, King Xerxes and his army were reported to have crossed the Bosporus in Turkey in 480 B.C.E. They used a pontoon bridge made of 300 boats. These bridges rarely lasted for more than a few days.

The Romans

Many of the Romans' bridges were wooden and have not survived. Others were made of stone, however, and some can still be seen today. The Romans perfected a new building technique involving an arch. This made a much stronger and safer bridge. They also used the arch to make aqueduct bridges that carried water into their towns. The discovery of a waterproof cement called *pozzolana* allowed them to make concrete for underwater foundations, and the development of the **coffer dam** became an essential technique for bridge-building.

The modern day

Bridge-building changed little from Roman times until the nineteenth century. Then, great changes were made, thanks to the availability of iron, steel, and reinforced concrete. Woven wire made it possible to build long suspension bridges. Other types of bridges include swing bridges, vertical lift bridges, and drawbridges, but the pillar and beam, arch, suspension, and coffer dam techniques are still used for most bridges today.

Building an arch

Arches in Roman bridges made them strong and safe. They were built like this:

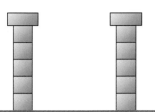

1. A column of stones formed a pier.

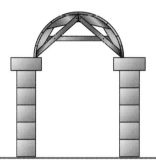

2. An arch-shaped wooden support was built between two columns.

3. Wedge-shaped stones were placed on top of the wooden support. When the arch was completed, the wooden supports were removed.

10,000 B.C.E.	400 B.C.E.	300 B.C.E.	1841 C.E.	1998
The first log bridges are used.	Pillar and beam bridges are used in the Middle East.	The Romans invent *pozzolana*, a waterproof cement.	The invention of woven iron cable makes possible the development of modern suspension bridges.	The world's longest bridge, the Akashi Kaikyo in Japan, is completed. It is 6,750 feet (2,060 meters) long.

Roads, 4000 B.C.E.

Soon after cities and towns began to form, around 4000 B.C.E., routes between them began to appear. Usually these roads were just simple dirt tracks. Historians think that Ur, an early city in the Middle East, had paved streets. If this is true, these would have been the world's first paved roads.

Roman roads

The Minoans of Crete built a limestone-paved road around 2000 B.C.E., and the ancient Egyptians and Babylonians also built roads. But the Romans were the greatest road builders of ancient times. Their roads were built to be so strong that some are still in use today. The **network** of roads the Romans left behind forms the basis of Europe's road and rail lines.

In all, the Romans constructed 29 major routes totaling over 50,000 miles (80,000 kilometers), all of which were linked to Rome. Once a country had been conquered, roads were built swiftly. These roads enabled armies to march quickly to trouble spots, but they were also used by traders and ordinary travelers.

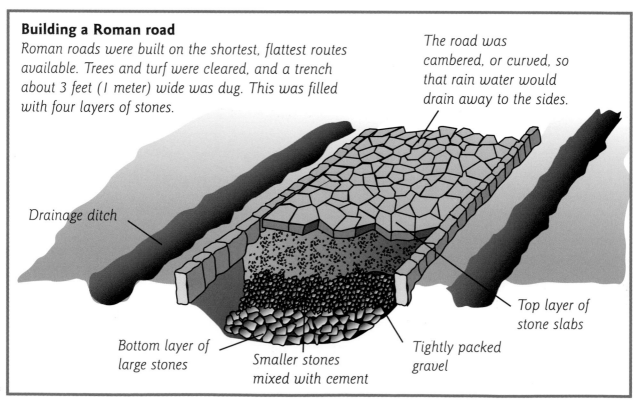

Building a Roman road
Roman roads were built on the shortest, flattest routes available. Trees and turf were cleared, and a trench about 3 feet (1 meter) wide was dug. This was filled with four layers of stones.

The road was cambered, or curved, so that rain water would drain away to the sides.

Drainage ditch

Bottom layer of large stones

Smaller stones mixed with cement

Tightly packed gravel

Top layer of stone slabs

Turnpikes

When the Roman **Empire** collapsed, its roads gradually fell into disrepair. Only in the mid-1700s did governments begin to make improvements in their roads. In Britain, **turnpike** companies maintained stretches of road but charged travelers to use them. In the United States, turnpike companies also maintained some roads. But when railroads were introduced in the nineteenth century, few roads made a profit, and many were turned over to local governments to run.

The arrival of fast-moving cars meant that existing roads, like this autobahn in Germany, had to be rapidly improved.

The road to the highway

Scottish road builder John Loudon McAdam (1756–1836) developed a method that was adopted throughout Europe. The roads were made of three layers of small stones placed over flattened and well-drained soil that was raised above the surrounding ground. After 1830, railroads became an increasingly popular way to travel, and many roads once again fell into disrepair.

The popularity of the bicycle and the arrival of motor transportation at the latter end of the nineteenth century forced governments to improve roads. Usually, a layer of tar or asphalt was placed over the existing surface and topped with stone chips to improve grip. Governments began to build highways with hard-wearing concrete surfaces ideal for use by fast-moving traffic. The first high-speed highway was built in Berlin between 1913 and 1921. Between the 1930s and 1960s, highway routes sprang up all over the world.

4000 B.C.E.	2000 B.C.E.	500 B.C.E.– 476 C.E.	1816	1913–1921
Paved streets may have been used in the city of Ur.	The Minoans build a limestone road in Crete.	The Romans build the finest roads in the ancient world.	John McAdam develops a method of building roads that is adopted throughout Europe.	The first high-speed highway is built in Berlin, Germany.

Wheel, 3500 B.C.E.

The wheel arrived in human history around 3500 B.C.E. in the Old World. However, the wheel was unknown to such New World civilizations as the Incas until Europeans arrived in the sixteenth century—5,000 years after it had been invented. Wheels would not have been much help on the narrow mountain paths used by the Incas.

The first wheel?

The first wheel may have been a potter's wheel. Such devices enabled clay containers to be made much more quickly. Historical records show that potter's wheels and ox-drawn carts arrived at around the same time—3500 B.C.E. Both came from the Middle Eastern civilizations of Mesopotamia and Sumeria.

It is likely that the wheel evolved from the roller. Rollers such as tree trunks had been used to move heavy loads like building stones and boats. Eventually, someone must have thought about putting the roller on another early invention, the sledge. This could be pulled along by animals, such as oxen, using a yoke. This technique was also used to pull plows over land used for farming.

A perfect circle

Because the wheel is circular, it can turn continuously. Only one small part of the wheel is in contact with the ground at any one time. But wheels also require a lot of skill to build. A carpenter would have to make a perfect circle and join the circle to the **axle** exactly at its midpoint. Any wheel not made accurately would make the cart it was attached to bounce around uncomfortably.

This magnificent seventh-century chariot belongs to the Assyrian King Assurbanipal. The sturdy wheels were strong enough to support a platform carrying four men. The chariot was harnessed to two horses.

The first wheels were made of three pieces of carved wood nailed to two connecting boards. Three pieces of wood were used because trees in the Middle East rarely grew trunks big enough to make an entire wheel. More improvements were made later. To make the wheel lighter, wood between the axle and outer rim was hollowed out to make spokes. The rim was also strengthened, first with another wooden strip and later with a thin copper band.

Trade became much easier as goods and people could be carried long distances more quickly. Contact with other tribes and civilizations also brought wealth, materials, and fresh ideas.

Essential invention

Other than transportation, the wheel has had other vital uses. Waterwheels helped **irrigate** some of the first farms, allowing crops to be grown on land that would previously never have sustained them. Waterwheels also powered flour mills. Before the invention of the steam engine thousands of years later, they also drove textile-making machinery in the first factories of the **Industrial Revolution.**

3500 B.C.E.	2000 B.C.E.	16th Century C.E.	1888
The wheel is invented in Mesopotamia and Sumeria.	Spokes were devised to make wheels lighter.	Europeans intoduce the wheel in North and South America.	John Dunlop invents the **pneumatic tire.**

In 1888, John Dunlop's son posed on the first bicycle to have pneumatic tires.

Sailing Ship, 3100 B.C.E.

As humans spread throughout the world, they made boats with whatever materials were available to them. In Europe, large trees were plentiful, so boats were usually made of hollowed-out logs. In Egypt, big trees were rare, so woven reeds from the papyrus plant were used. In the Middle East, boats were made of planks and inflated animal hides, and in North America they were often made of bark on a wooden frame. All of these vessels were powered by simple paddles.

The sail and oar

The first sails were probably used in Egyptian boats on the Nile in around 3100 B.C.E. A simple sail could catch the wind and push a boat against the river current. Square or rectangular sails were set at a right angle along a tall wooden pole called a mast.

Oars were invented around 1500 B.C.E. Unlike paddles, which are simply pushed into the water by the user, oars rest on a **pivot** at the side of the boat. This provides a more powerful push through the water. But it was expensive to hire people to work the oars. In general, warships were more willing to pay for the extra speed that oars could provide. But most trading vessels, eager to keep costs as low as possible, still relied on sails to get them from one place to another.

This wooden model from around 1300 B.C.E. shows the type of boat that would carry people and cargo up and down the Nile in Egypt.

Further developments

Over the centuries, boats grew sturdier and larger and bigger sails were used. A deep **keel** under the boat also balanced the weight of a tall mast. By Roman times, some ships had two masts and two or three sails.

Starting in about 1200 C.E., European vessels adopted the "lateen" sail used on Arab trading boats. It was triangular and could be set at an angle on the mast. This shape made it much easier for a ship to sail against the wind. Spanish and Portuguese sailors in the fifteenth and sixteenth centuries used lateen sails on their great voyages around the world.

By the 1800s, huge vessels with several masts and twelve or more sails would carry hundreds of passengers and thousands of tons of **cargo** around the globe. It would take 100 days to travel between Shanghai and London, but at the time this seemed remarkably swift. During the nineteenth and early twentieth centuries, steam-powered paddles, and then **propellers,** gradually replaced sails.

Vessels like this mid-nineteenth century clipper ship, which carried 700 passengers, were used until faster and more efficient steamships took over.

50,000 B.C.E.	5000 B.C.E.	3100 B.C.E.	1500 B.C.E.	13th Century C.E.
The first known boats—dugout canoes powered by paddles—are used.	Reed and wooden ships are built in Egypt and Mesopotamia.	The first sails are used on boats in the Nile River.	The oar is invented. It is three times more efficient than the paddle.	European ships adopt Arabic lateen sails. These make it easier for them to sail into the wind.

Horse Travel, 2000 B.C.E.

Horses were first harnessed to wheeled vehicles in around 2000 B.C.E. On a good level path, a four-wheeled horse-drawn wagon could cover 100 miles (160 kilometers) a day. Horse-drawn vehicles revolutionized warfare. A warrior on a chariot had a speed and flexibility that an ordinary foot soldier did not. The chariot itself could be used as a weapon if its wheels were fitted with sharp blades called scythes.

Horses allowed information to be carried quickly across a country or **empire.** A series of horses and riders could carry orders from a king, or news of a battle, up to 190 miles (300 kilometers) a day. Communication would not be faster until the nineteenth century.

Stirrups, reins, and saddles

The first known stirrups were used by the Scythians, who lived in what is now Turkey, around 380 B.C.E. These stirrups, probably made of leather, helped a rider to stay on the horse's back, using his feet and legs for support. Stirrups were not used in Europe until after Roman times. By about 300 B.C.E., the **Celts** of northern Europe were using reins and a bit to control their horses. This equipment took advantage of the fact that a horse runs with its head forward: if the head is pulled up, the horse will stop. The first saddles originated in China in the first century C.E.

This four-wheeled Sumerian wagon is drawn by two horses. It dates from around 2500 B.C.E.

Toward the 21st century

For nearly 2,000 years, **cavalry** was the most feared and effective weapon a commander could employ—until the twentieth century brought guided missiles, tanks, and modern aircraft. In the 1700s, horses pulled canal barges carrying the coal and factory goods that were vital to the success of the **Industrial Revolution.** In the nineteenth century, horse-drawn stagecoaches carried settlers to the new western territories. The first combine-harvesters of the early 1800s used teams of up to 30 horses to pull them through the fields.

The days of horse-drawn transportation came to an end with the discovery of **steam power** and the invention of the **internal combustion engine.** Cars, motorcycles, planes, and helicopters revolutionized transportation as we know it. Today, horses are still an essential way of carrying people and goods in many developing countries, but in the West, they are used mostly for leisure and sports.

When the United States expanded its borders in the nineteenth century, the stagecoach was one of the main methods of travel for people heading west to the new territories.

2000 B.C.E.	380 B.C.E.	300 B.C.E.	100 C.E.
Horses are first harnessed to wheeled vehicles.	The Scythians use stirrups for riding horses.	The Celts use reins and bits to control horses.	Saddles are used in China.

Submarine, 1620 C.E.

Submarines became one of the most influential weapons of the twentieth century, but their invention and development was slow in coming. Alexander the Great (356–323 B.C.E.) was said to have used some sort of submarine to defend his fleet from attacking divers, and there are records of diving bells being used as early as 200 B.C.E.

The twelve-man crew of Van Drebel's submarine rowed it down the Thames River from Westminster to Greenwich.

The first real submarine was invented by Dutchman Cornelius van Drebel. He based it on British mathematician William Bourne's ideas of a leather-clad craft that was driven through the water by oars. Van Drebel's invention was tested on the Thames River in London in 1620, with twelve men rowing eight miles (thirteen kilometers) from Westminster to Greenwich. It floated sixteen feet (five meters) underwater, and a tube to the surface gave the crew fresh air. But little more was heard of submarines for another 150 years.

The eighteenth century

War spurred on the submarine's development over the next 200 years. An inventor named David Bushnell built a submarine called the *Turtle*, which was used in an appempt to blow up a British warship in New York harbor in 1776, during the Revolutionary War. However, the attempt was not successful. The *Turtle* was a strange egg-shaped vessel, and it moved by turning a screw **propeller** by hand.

Submarines making use of air- or water-filled ballast tanks to take them above or below the surface were invented in 1801 by Robert Fulton. Electric motors were first used to power submarines in 1886. By the early twentieth century, submarines carried both **diesel** engines to drive them along the surface and electric engines to propel them underwater. The diesel engines were much cheaper to run, so they were used for long-distance travel.

Diesel and electrical engines were an efficient combination that tied in with another technological breakthrough—accurate, effective **torpedoes,** invented in 1866. The first use of **periscopes** around the same time meant that the submarine crew could see to attack from underwater. During World War I, from 1914 to 1918, German submarines called U-boats were so effective they almost won the war. One, named *U-35,* sank 324 **Allied** ships.

The introduction of **nuclear power** to submarines in 1954 meant they did not need air to power the engines. This gave these vessels an almost unlimited underwater range. In 1960, the American submarine U.S.S. *Triton* traveled underwater all the way around the world in twelve weeks. This, and the fact that submarines are not easily detected, means they are perfect carriers of nuclear missiles.

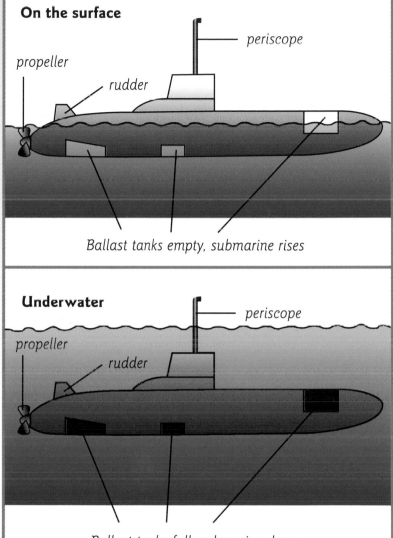

How a submarine works

Submarines rise or drop beneath the surface by flooding or emptying their ballast tanks. Taking in water makes the submarine heavier, so it sinks. Expelling the water by using compressed air makes the submarine lighter, so it rises to the surface.

On the surface

periscope

propeller

rudder

Ballast tanks empty, submarine rises

Underwater

periscope

propeller

rudder

Ballast tanks full, submarine drops

200 B.C.E.	1620 C.E.	1776	1886	1914–1918	1954
The first use of diving bells is recorded.	Cornelius van Drebel's oar-powered submarine makes its first voyage.	Submarines are first used in warfare.	Electric motors are first fitted to submarines.	The submarine is one of the most effective weapons of World War I.	Nuclear-powered submarines are introduced.

Steamship, 1783

For thousands of years, ships had been moved along by oars and sails, and seafarers were reluctant to change from these methods. The first steam-powered voyage took place in 1783. Marquis Jouffroy d'Abbans took his boat, *Peryscaphe,* out onto the Saône River in Lyon, France. For fifteen minutes, a wheezing, billowing steam engine drove a set of paddles that moved *Peryscaphe* along. The trip came to an abrupt end when the boat shook to pieces.

In 1787, American inventor John Fitch ran a steamboat on the Delaware River. In 1807, Robert Fulton built the first passenger-carrying steamship, the *Clermont,* which ran between New York City and Albany. The *Clermont,* belching smoke and flames, steamed along against the tide and wind, making its 150-mile (240-kilometer) journey in 32 hours.

Robert Fulton's Clermont *was the first steamship to make regular passenger trips. Its engine drove two paddle wheels on either side of the vessel.*

Steamships at sea

The first seagoing steamship was built by John and Robert Stevens. In 1809, their boat, the *Phoenix,* took thirteen days to travel between New York and Philadelphia. By 1838, regular Atlantic crossings were being made, although early steamships usually carried both a steam engine and sails—this way they could make good use of the wind, and they were prepared in case the engine broke down.

At first, steam engines drove ships with huge paddle wheels—one on each side, or one at the back. In 1835, the **propeller** took over as the better means of **propulsion.** Paddles were more easily damaged and lifted out of the water when the sea was rough. However, they remained popular with river steamships until well into the twentieth century because they could travel in very shallow water.

Engine improvements during the nineteenth century demonstrated that using steam was better than using sails. The first steamboats used wood for fuel, but in 1818 Robert Stevens showed that coal was much more efficient. The **steam turbine** was developed by Charles Parsons in 1884. This machine forced high-pressure steam over turbine blades that turned a propeller shaft, considerably increasing the power of the engine and the speed of the ship. By the end of the century, ships were also using two, three, and even four propellers. These would keep a propeller-driven steamship from being stranded if its propeller shaft broke.

Today, most ocean-going ships are still powered by steam turbines, and some use **nuclear power** to generate their steam.

When it was launched in 1858, Isambard Kingdom Brunel's Great Eastern was the largest vessel ever built. Like many other early ocean-going steamships, it also carried a full set of sails.

1783	1787	1807	1819	1838	1884
Marquis Jouffroy d'Abbans makes the first steam-powered voyage in the *Peryscaphe*.	John Fitch sails a small steamboat on the Delaware River.	Robert Fulton introduces the first steamship passenger service, between New York City and Albany.	The *Savannah* crosses the Atlantic, although it uses its sails for much of the journey.	Regular steamship service is in place across the Atlantic.	Charles Parsons invents the steam turbine.

Balloon, 1783

The first attempts at flying were usually heroic leaps from tall buildings or cliffs, with aspiring birdmen wearing makeshift wings made of feathers or wood. These experiments were usually fatal. But the Chinese were able to fly humans on the front of giant kites as early as the sixth century C.E. They could be said to have invented the first hang gliders.

Experiments

In the royal courtroom of the king of Portugal, João V, in 1709, Father Bartolomeu de Gusmão demonstrated how a small balloon could rise up to the ceiling. His invention was based on the fact that hot air rises. The balloon carried a small candle that heated the air inside it, causing it to rise. But, fearing his curtains would be set on fire, the king ordered a guard to shoot the balloon down.

The first manned balloon flight, in November 1783, was in a balloon built by the Montgolfier brothers.

Later that century, two wealthy French brothers, Joseph and Étienne Montgolfier, watched flakes of ash rise above a blazing fire and noted that upended paper bags floated even higher. So in June 1783, they demonstrated a huge hot air balloon in Annonay, France. It was made from cloth lined with paper and measured 35 feet (11 meters) across. Beneath the balloon, on the ground, was a fire that heated up the air that would carry the balloon into the sky.

The huge unmanned balloon rose 3,000 feet (1,000 meters) into the air and landed more than 1.5 miles (2.4 kilometers) away. The next flight, three months later, carried a duck, a sheep, and a rooster; a human volunteer went up a month later. Scientist Pilâtre de Rozier was the first man to travel in a balloon, although it was connected to the ground with a rope. The first free-floating flight took place on November 21. De Rozier and a French soldier, Marquis d'Arlandes, flew 5.5 miles (9 kilometers) through the air, for nearly half an hour.

Bad invention
Hydrogen was far more efficient than hot air, but it had one great disadvantage—it burned very easily. In the 1920s and 1930s, great hydrogen-filled airships were built to ferry passengers across the Atlantic Ocean. In 1937, the German-built *Hindenburg* was coming in to land at Lakehurst, New Jersey, when it burst into flames. The huge airship was completely destroyed in 30 seconds, and 35 passengers and crew were killed.

Discovery of hydrogen

The Montgolfiers' rival, Jacques Charles, flew a hydrogen balloon in August of 1783. His was made of rubber and silk and filled with hydrogen, a gas that is lighter than air and does not need to be heated. On its first unmanned flight, his balloon drifted from Paris to Gonesse, 15 miles (24 kilometers) away. When it landed, it was hacked to pieces by frightened farmers. A couple of weeks after the Montgolfiers' first manned flight, Charles took himself and another passenger on a 27-mile (43-kilometer) journey.

Army commanders, such as Napoleon, realized that balloons would be excellent observation platforms during battles. But balloons could not be steered and depended on air currents to move along. Today, balloons are most often used for pleasure, or by **meteorologists** to study the weather.

1709	1783	1785	1937	1978	1999
Father Bartolomeu de Gusmão demonstrates the idea of the hot air balloon to the Portuguese court.	The Montgolfier brothers invent the first hot air balloon. Jacques Charles invents the hydrogen balloon.	A balloon first crosses the English Channel.	The *Hindenburg* bursts into flames, killing 36 people.	The first hot air balloon crosses the Atlantic Ocean.	A balloon flies nonstop all the way around the world.

Steam Locomotive, 1804

The first steam engine was invented in Egypt around 2,000 years ago, though it was not until the early eighteenth century that the idea was put to practical use. Building on the work of Denis Papin and Thomas Savery, an English inventor named Thomas Newcomen made a machine in 1712 called the Atmospheric Steam-Engine. Designed to pump water from coal mines, it used steam produced by boiling water to drive a **piston** that could be rapidly and repeatedly raised and lowered.

In 1781, Scottish instrument-maker James Watt devised a way of transforming the piston's up-and-down motion to circular motion so that it could turn a wheel. Steam engines were immediately put to use driving factory machinery, helping to make Britain the nineteenth century's richest and most powerful nation.

Trevithick's locomotive, Catch me who can, *was a sensation in London in 1808 but failed to attract financial backing to further develop the idea.*

Trains and steam engines

Rails for carrying wheeled vehicles had been used by the ancient Greeks to haul boats over the narrow **isthmus** of Corinth. They were also used in European mines from as early as the fifteenth century. When Newcomen was inventing his steam engine, rails carrying horse-drawn coal wagons were a common feature in British mines.

Richard Trevithick was the first inventor to put steam engines and trains together. In 1804, he built a locomotive that carried ten tons of iron and 70 men along the train track at Pen-y-Darren in South Wales. In 1808, he brought a locomotive called *Catch me who can* to London to raise money to develop the idea. Though he made a major sensation, Trevithick attracted no backers. He gave up his work on locomotives, emigrated to Peru to work on steam-powered mining pumps, and died in poverty in 1833.

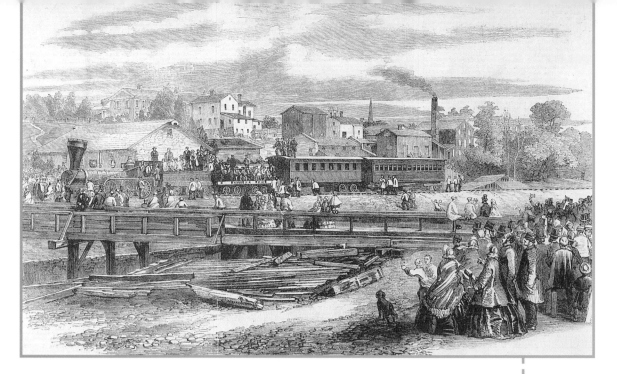

The coal industry

Trevithick's idea was developed in the coal mining industry. In 1825, engineer George Stephenson completed a 25-mile (40-kilometer) rail line between the coal-mining town of Darlington and the port of Stockton, in the northeast of England. A steam train of his own design hauled coal from the mine to the coast, where it could be taken around the country by boat. It also carried paying passengers.

The first train of the Atlantic and Great Western railroad arrived at Jamestown, New York, from New York City in 1860.

In 1830, Stephenson completed the first intercity line, between Liverpool and Manchester. The line had a two-way track and ran on a daily schedule. The locomotives that pulled the carriages at 30 miles (50 kilometers) per hour were Stephenson's, too. His design, the *Rocket,* had won a competition to find the best locomotive available.

Within twenty years, rail travel had begun to spread around the world. Rail provided cheap and fast travel over long distances for both goods and people. Today, steam trains have mostly been replaced by electric- or **diesel**-powered locomotives.

0 C.E.	1712	1804	1825	1869
The first steam engine is invented in Egypt.	Thomas Newcomen's Atmospheric Steam-Engine pumps water from mines.	Richard Trevithick runs a locomotive on the rail line at Pen-y-Darren in Wales.	George Stephenson builds the first public railroad, from Darlington to Stockton, England.	The first transcontinental railroad, linking the east coast to the west, is completed.

Bicycle, 1817

The first recognizable bicycle arrived in 1817. It was called a draisienne, after its German inventor, Baron Karl von Drais. His machine had two spoked iron wheels connected by a crossbar, and a steering device. There were no pedals, but a rider could reach a speed of 9 miles (15 kilometers) per hour by pushing along with the feet. A journey that would have taken a day's walk could now be done in two or three hours.

In many ways, the draisienne looked like a modern bicycle, although it would be years before the bike we know today was perfected. In 1842, Scottish blacksmith Kirkpatrick MacMillan made a bicycle with pedals similar to the **treadles** that power sewing machines. MacMillan rode his bicycle 40 miles (64 kilometers) between Dumfries and Glasgow to prove its worth, but it never caught on. He lacked the ability to successfully publicize and exploit the idea.

Setting the pace

Next came the velocipede, a French word that means "swift foot." Invented by father and son Pierre and Ernest Michaux in 1861, it had pedals attached to a large front wheel. It was sometimes known as the "boneshaker" because it was so uncomfortable to ride. Britain's James Starley developed their idea further in 1870, attaching his pedal directly to a much bigger front wheel. His machine was known as the "penny-farthing" because the two British coins of those names were relatively similar in proportion to the front and back wheels. It was difficult and dangerous to use but reached an impressive speed of 20 miles (32 kilometers) per hour.

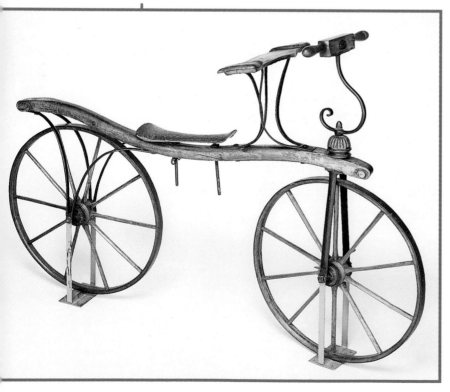

The draisienne, or hobby-horse, reached speeds of 9 miles (15 kilometers) per hour.

And finally...

The final step in the development of the bicycle came in 1879, when Harry J. Lawson fitted a chain to connect his pedals to the back wheel. This idea was taken up by a nephew of James Starley's named John K. Starley. In 1885, he produced the Rover Safety bicycle. It returned to von Drais's original idea of two wheels of the same size, making it much safer to ride. This final design breakthrough produced a machine similar to a modern-day bicycle.

Modern day bicycles are much lighter and stronger than earlier models. This racing bike, seen at the Sydney Olympics in 2000, is one example.

Further refinements, such as brakes, **sprung** saddles for extra comfort, lighter frames, and John Dunlop's much speedier **pneumatic tires,** made bicycles an even greater success. They were cheap and pleasant to ride. They made travel so much easier that they soon became enormously popular.

In the early twentieth century, cars and motorcycles offered even easier and speedier ways of getting from one place to another, and the popularity of the bicycle soon faded. But a combination of road **congestion,** pollution, and interest in exercise and fitness has meant that the bike is almost as popular now as it was in its brief heyday 100 years ago.

1817	1842	1861	1870	1885
The first bicycle, the draisienne, is introduced.	Kirkpatrick MacMillan's bicycle is the first to have pedals.	The velocipede is made with pedals attached directly to the front wheel.	James Starley develops the "penny-farthing."	John K. Starley introduces the Rover Safety bicycle, with a chain linking the pedals to the wheel.

Subway, 1863

The first underground railroad line in the world was built in London in 1863 as a response to traffic **congestion.** It also provided transportation into the city for **commuters** who lived in the suburbs. It was called the Metropolitan Railway and stretched from Paddington Station to Farringdon, 3.75 miles (6 kilometers) away. There were several other stations along the route.

The line was built using the "cut and cover" technique of tunnel building. A broad trench was dug in the ground and supported by brick walls, the track was laid, and then the tunnel was covered over.

The Metropolitan Line used steam trains. Ventilation holes were regularly spaced along its length, and special **condensers** collected some of the smoke that billowed from the trains. It was a dirty, unpleasant experience, but it was extremely popular.

Marc Isambard Brunel's tunnel shield made it possible to burrow under rivers and paved the way for the deep tunnels that were built for the London underground rail system.

Tunnels
Modern tunneling began in 1818, when Marc Isambard Brunel invented a tunneling device inspired by the shipworm *Terado navalis,* which burrowed into wood. Called the "tunnel shield," it was a box-shaped iron case with cells for 33 miners to dig away in relative safety. A brick lining was built around the hole they made. Peter Barlow and James Henry Greathead developed this idea and used cast-iron segments rather than bricks to build the lining of the tunnel. This method was used to make the deep tunnels of London's underground rail system.

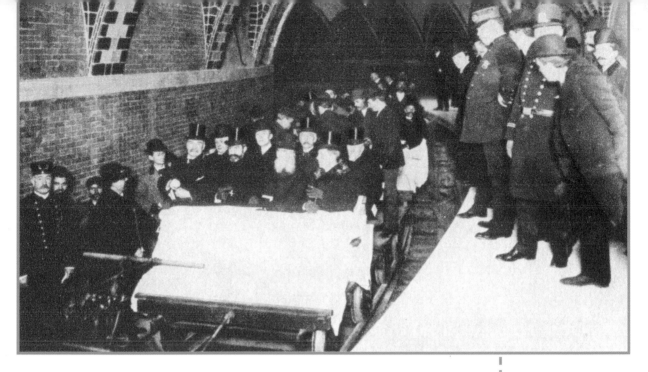

Electric trains

In 1879, Werner von Siemens unveiled an electric train at the Berlin Exhibition. Battery-powered trains had been used before, with limited success, but Siemens' train took its power directly from a "live" rail on the track. This means the rail had electricity running though it. It was fast, efficient, relatively quick, and it was clean.

A deep underground line called the "City and South London Railway" was built in London for this new type of train. Its fourteen electric locomotives each pulled three carriages and could travel up and down the tracks at a rate of one train every four minutes. Each train could carry 100 passengers, and in its first year, the line carried five million people.

Underground systems were then built in major cities all around the world. Paris opened its Métro in 1900, and New York began its subway service in 1904. These trains are still the quickest way to get around many major cities.

The opening of the New York subway in 1904 saw the mayor of New York taking a tour of the first completed section.

1818	1863	1879	1897	1900	1904
Marc Isambard Brunel invents the tunnel shield.	The world's first underground rail service, the Metropolitan Line, opens in London.	Werner von Siemens unveils an electric-powered train at the Berlin Exhibition.	The Boston subway system, the first in the United States, opens.	The Paris Métro opens.	The New York subway system opens.

Motorcycle, 1885

Invented at about the same time as the car, the motorcycle is essentially a bicycle with a motor attached to it. The first motorcycle was built in 1869 and used **steam power.** The weight of the **boiler** and steam engine mounted on a French velocipede bicycle must have made it very unstable. In 1884, L. D. Copeland of Philadelphia began manufacturing steam-powered tricycles. The third wheel made these less likely to topple over.

Motorcycles and gasoline

The first motorcycle with a gasoline engine was made by car inventor Gottlieb Daimler in 1885. It was a heavy, clumsy-looking vehicle with the engine mounted high on the bike. In 1894, the German company Hildebrand and Wolfmüller began to make the "Motorrad"—the first factory-produced bike.

By the early 1900s, the design had settled into one we would recognize today. The wheels were the same size, the engine was mounted low on the body to make the bike more stable, and the back wheel was driven with a chain or belt. The sidecar was introduced in 1903, and **twist-grip throttles** were invented in 1904. These allowed the rider to control the speed of the bike by hand rather than by foot. By 1914, the bike could go as fast as 95 miles (150 kilometers) per hour. When World War I began in 1914, speedy motorcyclists were soon used to carry messages to and from army headquarters.

Because they were inexpensive and easy to use, the first motorcycles, like this factory-produced model, were at least as popular as cars.

A versatile machine

Motorcycles were cheaper to buy than cars, cheaper to run, and easier to take care of. They were also faster and easier to maneuver, but they were much more dangerous. Their small size made them difficult for motorists to see and gave the rider no protection from other vehicles or the weather. But in Britain and many other countries, motorcycles were more popular than cars until the 1950s.

After World War II, there was a huge population increase in Europe and North America. Cars were more suitable for families, and motorcycles became less popular. Scooters became very popular with teenagers during the 1950s, as did mopeds. Similar to early motorcycles because they were essentially bicycles with motors, mopeds were originally developed during World War II. They were useful in hit-and-run raids because they could be carried on a soldier's back.

In more recent times, increased traffic **congestion** has made the motorcycle more popular—it can weave in and out of city traffic jams. Police forces and delivery companies still use motorcycles for these reasons.

Popular with both the police and motorcycle gangs, the Harley Davidson is one of the most admired motorcycles of the twentieth century. The first models were built in 1903.

1869	1884	1885	1894	1903
The first steam-powered motorcycle is introduced.	A steam-powered tricycle is invented.	Gottlieb Daimler produces the first gasoline-engine motorcycle.	Hildebrand and Wolfmüller manufacture the "Motorrad." the first factory-produced bike.	The sidecar is invented.

Car, 1886

Inventors had been trying to come up with a "horseless carriage" for centuries. A primitive steam-powered cart may have been driven around China in 1662. French inventor Nicolas-Joseph Cugnot designed a lumbering, steam-powered carriage in 1770. It had a huge **boiler** at the front and looked like a giant ant.

Fuel and the internal combustion engine

In the early nineteenth century, new fuels such as coal gas became available. The **internal combustion engine** was developed to make use of this gas. But the real breakthrough came when German Karl Benz produced an internal combustion engine that used gasoline, an unwanted by-product of the oil **refinery** industry.

Internal combustion engine

An internal combustion engine works by exploding fuel to move a **piston.** The moving piston rotates a **crankshaft** that can be made to turn the car wheels. The first was built by a Frenchman, Étienne Lenoir. He used a converted steam engine that exploded a mixture of air and coal gas to drive a piston. In 1876, Nikolaus Otto and Eugen Langen invented an engine using natural gas for power. In 1885, Karl Benz produced an engine that used gasoline instead of natural gas. He also discovered that an electric spark was the best way to ignite his fuel. His engine was much lighter than those using natural gas, making it more suitable for a road vehicle.

In 1885, Karl Benz fitted a gasoline engine to a three-wheeled carriage. He **patented** his invention in 1886, the same year that two other German inventors, Gottlieb Daimler and Wilhelm Maybach, unveiled their four-wheeled motorcar, which used the same type of engine. The first cars could travel only a little faster than a horse. By the turn of the century, they could go as fast as 100 miles (160 kilometers) per hour.

The internal combustion engine was soon put to use in many forms of transportation, such as the motorcycle, bus, and truck, as well as farming machinery such as the tractor and **threshing** machine. It was also used in airplanes and helicopters.

Improvements

Henry Ford decided to make cars in the millions, giving ordinary people the freedom to go anywhere, at any time. Today, there are about 500 million cars in daily use around the world.

Since the birth of the car, there have been many improvements. In 1892, the **diesel** engine was invented. Later, front-wheel steering instead of back-wheel steering was used, brakes were fitted to all four wheels, and gears and wheel **suspension** improved. Since the 1970s, efforts have been made to redesign cars to cut down the pollution their engines cause, by making them produce cleaner exhaust. But even with all the changes, the basic design of a motor car is still fundamentally the same as it was 100 years ago.

Ford's Model T *was the first cheap, mass-produced car. Fifteen million of them were built on production lines like this one in Detroit, seen here in 1913.*

1859	1885	1886	1892	1909
Étienne Lenoir invents the internal combustion engine.	Karl Benz makes the first gasoline-driven internal combustion engine.	Karl Benz patents the first gasoline-driven car. Daimler and Maybach produce a four-wheeled car.	Rudolf Diesel patents the diesel engine.	Henry Ford invents the production line to mass-produce cars.

Airplane, 1903

On December 17, 1903, two brothers named Wilbur and Orville Wright took their gasoline-engine plane *Flyer 1* into the air at Kitty Hawk, North Carolina. This first manned, powered flight was one of the great events of the twentieth century. Although the flights on that day lasted no more than 60 seconds, the possibilities the *Flyer* offered were phenomenal.

Wilbur Wright (1867–1912) and Orville Wright (1871–1948)

The Wright brothers grew up in Dayton, Ohio. They began their careers editing and printing a local newspaper, the Dayton *West Side News*. They also opened a business that repaired, sold, and manufactured bicycles. Both enterprises helped finance their flying machine project. Wilbur died of **typhoid fever** in 1912, but Orville lived a long, prosperous life. The *Flyer* project cost the Wrights only $1,000. Orville eventually made over $500,000 from his invention, so it was an extremely successful investment.

The Wrights jealously guarded their claim to be the first people to fly. When the Smithsonian Institution in Washington, D.C. suggested that they might not have made the first powered flight, Wilbur sent *Flyer 1* to be displayed at the Science Museum in London instead. The Smithsonian was only allowed to have it back if they promised never again to contest the Wrights' claim to be the first people to fly.

The first real breakthrough in aircraft design came in the early nineteenth century. A wealthy British inventor, Sir George Cayley, spent much of his life making **gliders.** He built his first successful one in 1804, and by 1853 had made one big enough to carry someone 600 feet (183 meters) in the air.

In 1848, another British inventor, John Stringfellow, made a very short and shaky flight in a steam-powered flying machine. So did French engineer Clement Ader and American Hiram Maxim in the 1890s. In 1896, American professor Samuel P. Langley built an unmanned steam-powered model plane that was a sensation. The United States government gave him $50,000, a huge amount in those days, to develop it further for the army. However, his full-sized flying machines were unable to fly.

The Wright brothers

The Wright brothers were inspired to conquer the air by the death of Otto Lilienthal in a flying accident in 1896. Otto was one of two brothers who were making test flights with gliders in Germany. The Wrights read about the work of Cayley and the Lilienthals and started to work on improving existing designs.

Cooperating with their friend, engineer Octave Chanute, they built a series of gliders to test which aircraft shapes and control **mechanisms** worked best. They designed their own **propellers** and used the newly developed gasoline engine for power. Because this kind of engine was lighter and more powerful than previously available power sources, it was capable of lifting itself, the plane, and a passenger into the air.

By 1905 they had built *Flyer III*. It could stay in the air for 40 minutes. It could also fly relatively complex maneuvers, such as a figure eight. They took out **patents** for their machine and sold it to the United States Army and to French manufacturers. The airplane became one of the most influential inventions of the century. It revolutionized travel, cutting journey times between countries from days or weeks to mere hours. In warfare, troops could now be attacked from the sky as well as from the ground, and bombers had the power to bring destruction to cities hundreds of miles away from the fighting.

As Wilbur Wright runs behind him, Orville Wright makes the first successful powered flight. Flyer I was made of wood covered with cotton cloth. The twelve-horsepower engine turned two large wooden propellers.

1804	1848	1853	1891–1896	1903
Sir George Cayley makes the first successful glider.	John Stringfellow makes a flight in a steam-powered plane.	Cayley's glider makes a successful flight with a person on board.	Otto and Gustav Lilienthal make hundreds of pioneering glider flights, until Otto is killed in a flying accident.	The Wright brothers make the first manned, powered flight.

Jet, 1930

A hundred years ago, the fastest way to get from New York to London was by steamship. The trip took over a week. Today, the journey can be made by a **supersonic** jet airliner in an extraordinary three hours.

The jet engine

The first airplanes used **propellers** to pull them through the air. Some aircraft still use propellers today. But to go faster and higher, plane builders use a jet engine.

Frank Whittle, an **apprentice** in Britain's Royal Air Force (RAF), designed a working jet engine in the 1920s. He called it a "turbojet." The RAF wasn't interested in his jet, so he **patented** the idea himself in 1930. But by 1935, the British government feared they would soon be at war with Germany, so they arranged to go ahead with work on Whittle's jet engine. New metal **alloys** had been developed that could withstand the high temperatures generated by a continually running jet engine. Whittle had developed a full-size working engine by 1937. In 1941, the *Gloster Meteor,* a jet aircraft using this engine, took to the skies.

How a jet works
Turbojets like this one are used by all the fastest aircraft.

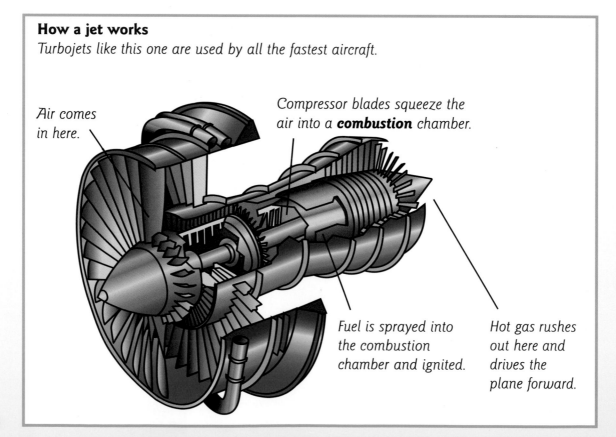

Air comes in here.

Compressor blades squeeze the air into a **combustion** chamber.

Fuel is sprayed into the combustion chamber and ignited.

Hot gas rushes out here and drives the plane forward.

Not knowing of Whittle's work, German engineer Hans Joachim Pabst von Ohain had patented his own jet engine in 1935. The German government was eager for von Ohain to develop his idea, because it would be a very effective weapon. It was a great success. Although Whittle invented the first jet engine, the first jet plane to actually fly was the *Heinkel He-178*, in August 1939.

The Germans introduced several jet **combat aircraft** during World War II. The deadliest was the *Messerschmitt Me-262*, a twin-engine fighter plane that was devastatingly effective against **Allied** warplanes.

After the war ended in 1945, another war seemed possible between Russia and the United States. This spurred more research into jet aircraft. In 1947, test pilot Chuck Yeager flew a rocket-propelled craft called the *Bell X-1* faster than the speed of sound, or 760 miles (1,225 kilometers) per hour. By the early 1960s, jet fighters such as the British *Lightning*, the American *Phantom*, and Russian *Mig-21* could all fly at twice this speed—covering a mile in less than three seconds.

*Some modern **military** jets, such as this F-3 Tornado, can change the position of their wings. Here, the wings are swept back—the best position for high-speed flight.*

1930	1935	1939	1941	1947
Frank Whittle patents the turbojet engine.	Hans Joachim Pabst von Ohain patents his own jet engine design.	The *Heinkel He-178*, the world's first jet aircraft, takes to the sky.	A British jet aircraft, the *Gloster Meteor*, makes its first flight.	Chuck Yeager flies the *Bell X-1* faster than the speed of sound.

Single-Rotor Helicopter, 1939

The idea of a wingless vehicle, thrust through the air by a revolving rotor, has been around for at least 1,600 years. The ancient Chinese had a spinning toy that flew straight into the air, called a "flying top." Italian artist Leonardo da Vinci sketched out an idea for a "flying screw" in 1480. It resembled the idea of helicopter design, but he mistakenly imagined that a person would be able to turn the rotor fast enough to lift it into the air.

Early twentieth-century attempts

The arrival of the **internal combustion engine** enabled the helicopter's development. In 1907, Frenchman Paul Cornu managed to get his **prototype** helicopter to take off. It wobbled six feet (1.8 meters) in the air for a hair-raising twenty seconds. When the engine cut out, it crashed to the ground and collapsed.

In 1923, Spanish inventor Juan de la Cierva flew an "autogiro," a strange helicopter-plane combination. This had a **propeller** at the front, like most aircraft of that era, but instead of wings, it had long flapping rotors. As the propeller pulled it along, the rotors spun and lifted it into the air. These rotors were hinged and could move up and down, allowing the pilot to control the direction of flight.

In 1938, legendary German test pilot Hanna Reitsch made a vertical landing of Focke's FA-61 inside the Berlin Olympic Stadium, demonstrating the helicopter's great advantage over the airplane.

The first real helicopters

The Germans developed the first real helicopter, Professor Heinrich Focke's *Focke-Achgelis FA-61*. It first flew in 1936. It had the shape of a plane, but instead of wings, there were two rotors held above the body of the plane. It could take off and land vertically and could hover in the air.

In the United States, Russian immigrant and helicopter designer Igor Sikorsky was watching these developments closely. In 1939, he took his own helicopter, the *VS-300,* into the air. It had all the features of most helicopters today. A single main rotor was placed behind the pilot, with another smaller one on the tail.

Helicopters were first used as **military** aircraft by the U.S. Navy in 1943. They were perfect for rescue missions, plucking sailors from the sea, or delivering and collecting soldiers and supplies in hard-to-reach places. Since the 1960s, helicopters fitted with missiles and machine guns have been used to attack infantry and tanks.

400 C.E.	1480	1907	1923	1936	1939
The Chinese invent a "flying top" toy.	Leonardo da Vinci sketches a "flying screw."	Paul Cornu flies his prototype helicopter for twenty seconds.	Juan de la Cierva flies an autogiro.	Professor Heinrich Focke's twin-rotor *Focke-Achgelis FA-61* makes its first flight.	Igor Sikorsky makes his first flight in the VS-300, the first single-rotor helicopter.

Hovercraft, 1955

The concept of a hovercraft, a vehicle that floats on a cushion of air, has been around since the seventeenth century. British inventor John Thornycroft worked on the idea in the 1870s, but he did not have an engine light enough and strong enough to power his design. The hovercraft had to wait for the invention of the **internal combustion engine** before it could be properly developed.

Christopher Cockerell

British inventor Christopher Cockerell was the first to build a working hovercraft. His initial design involved a combination of empty cans of cat food and coffee and a vacuum cleaner motor that had been altered to blow rather than suck. Cockerell's model clearly showed that a vessel could be lifted up by a cushion of air, and he **patented** it in 1955.

Next, he built a radio-controlled model. Government officials in 1956 thought it was such a sensation they ordered it to be kept secret and developed as a weapon. But the navy thought it was a plane and the air force thought it was a boat. Both felt the other should take responsibility for it, and the army wasn't interested at all. After three years of debate, Cockerell was allowed to take his invention to aircraft manufacturers to see what they could do with it.

Cockerell's SR.N1 was the world's first working hovercraft. The machine's abilities to travel quickly over water and to move from land to water with ease caused a sensation.

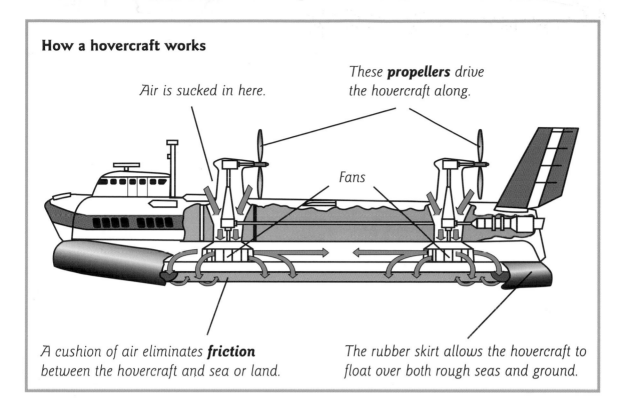

How a hovercraft works

Air is sucked in here.

These **propellers** drive the hovercraft along.

Fans

A cushion of air eliminates **friction** between the hovercraft and sea or land.

The rubber skirt allows the hovercraft to float over both rough seas and ground.

SR.N1

The first working hovercraft was built in 1959 by helicopter manufacturers Saunders Roe. They called it *SR.N1,* and Cockerell demonstrated its unique ability to travel smoothly between land and sea by driving it off the beach at Dover, England and across the English Channel to Calais, France.

The *SR.N1* worked only when the ground or sea it traveled over was very flat. This issue was solved when inventor C. H. Latimer-Needham devised a rubberized "skirt" that raised the hovercraft higher off the ground. This enabled the hovercraft to plow through choppy seas and over rough ground much more effectively.

Although hovercraft are now found all over the world, they never became as widely used as people imagined. Trains, boats, cars, and planes still do their jobs at least as well as a hovercraft.

1955	**1959**	**1961**	**1968**
After building a working model the previous year, Christopher Cockerell patents his hovercraft design.	The first full-size hovercraft is built. Cockerell pilots it across the English Channel.	C. H. Latimer-Needham invents a rubber skirt that allows hovercraft to travel on sea in rough weather.	Hovercraft passenger and car service across the English Channel begins.

Supertanker, 1956

Supertankers, officially known as "Ultra Large Crude Carriers," are among the biggest mobile objects ever built. The *Seawise Giant,* for example, would be taller than the twin towers of the World Trade Center in New York if it could be placed upright on its **stern.**

The first oil tanker

The first oil tanker was built in 1886, a year after the invention of the gasoline-powered **internal combustion engine.** Gasoline comes from crude oil, or oil in its natural state in the ground. Much of the world's supply is found in remote parts of the world, such as the Middle East, Alaska, and Siberia. By the 1930s, gasoline was in great demand. Although pipelines can be built to move oil from where it is found to where it is needed, the most economical way of transporting it is by sea.

An international crisis led to the creation of the first supertankers. The Suez Canal in Egypt links the Mediterranean Sea with the Red Sea. Without this canal, tankers traveling from the oil-rich Middle Eastern nations would have to go all the way around Africa to get to Europe or the United States. In 1956, and again between 1967 and 1975, the canal was closed because of wars between Egypt and other nations.

Many supertankers are too big for ports. This one is unloading its cargo of crude oil at a "single point mooring" (SPM). Oil unloaded here is carried by pipeline to a **refinery.**

Practical issues

Around this time, new shipbuilding techniques were being developed. Oil companies were able to have huge oil tankers built to carry more oil per trip, thus cutting the cost of transporting it, especially if they had to go all the way around Africa. Large prefabricated sections could be welded together, making construction much easier and quicker.

Tankers are very simple vessels. The engine and crew quarters are in the stern, where any fire would be less likely to spread to the highly **inflammable** oil. The **cargo** holds, where the oil is kept, are separated by many bulkheads, or partitions, to keep the liquid cargo from forming waves inside the **hull.** Such wave motion with thousands of tons of oil could cause serious damage to the tanker.

Although vessels like this supertanker are huge, they are really very simple to sail and operate. These ships need only small crews.

Risk of pollution

The history of supertankers is littered with accidents. In 1989, for example, the supertanker *Exxon Valdez* ran aground in Alaska. It leaked oil for two days, polluting 1,100 miles (1,770 kilometers) of coastline and killing many thousands of sea birds. There is a great deal of public concern about the safety of supertankers. Today, a typical supertanker can carry up to 40 million gallons of oil (about 600,000 tons, or 610,000 metric tons). On board, computers monitor the location and direction of the ship, and collision-avoidance **radar** continually monitors the possibility of a crash with other ships.

1885	1886	1956	1978	1989
The invention of the gasoline-powered internal combustion engine puts gasoline in demand.	The first oil tanker is built.	The first supertankers are built following the closure of the Suez Canal.	The *Amoco Cadiz* sinks off the French coast, causing terrible pollution.	An oil spill from the *Exxon Valdez* pollutes huge parts of the Alaskan coastline.

Jumbo Jet, 1969

Jet aircraft were developed during World War II. The first ones were very expensive to build and fly. The British *de Havilland Comet*, the first jet airliner, began carrying passengers in 1952. However, two years later two of the jets tore apart in the air, so it was grounded for several years.

In the United States, the Boeing company built a bigger and faster airliner called the 707. It was a four-engine jet that could take up to 180 passengers across the Atlantic at 600 miles (965 kilometers) per hour. Boeing knew that bigger planes would be even more profitable, because more paying passengers meant more money for fuel.

The bigger the better

In 1966, Boeing unveiled plans for the Boeing 747, quickly named the "Jumbo" because of its huge size. It made its first flight in 1969 and began to carry fare-paying passengers in 1970. It could carry between 385 and 500 passengers up to 8,000 miles (13,000 kilometers).

A jumbo jet has four "turbofan" engines that combine powerful **propulsion** with low fuel consumption. They are also relatively quiet and cause less pollution than conventional turbojet engines. Their low fuel consumption also means that jumbo jets are ideal for long-distance journeys. They can fly between Chicago and Tokyo, for example, without stopping to refuel.

Jumbo jets have been so successful that airports have had to lengthen their runways and redesign their passenger facilities to accommodate these huge aircraft.

This Boeing 747 carries a NASA space shuttle. The shuttle made its first flight when it was launched from the back of a Jumbo jet.

Today's jumbo jets

Today, jumbo jet engines burn even less fuel, cause less air and noise pollution, and are controlled by digital electronics and computer displays. The first 747s had a mind-boggling 971 dials, lights, and gauges on the control panels. Now there are only 365.

Jumbo jets also make up a third of the world's **cargo**-carrying aircraft. They take troops to trouble spots around the world and carry space shuttles for NASA. In 1990, two uniquely modified 747s replaced the 707s that had carried U.S. presidents since 1962.

Jumbo facts

- Each jumbo jet is made of more than six million parts.
- Jumbo jets have earned Boeing more than $100 billion.
- In 30 years of flying the world's air routes, the 747 has carried enough passengers to equal a quarter of the world's population.
- Each jet has eighteen tires—sixteen on the central fuselage, and two on the nose wheel.
- The tail of a jumbo jet is 63 feet, 8 inches (19.41 meters)—the same size as a six-story building.

1952	1963	1969	1977	1990
The *de Havilland Comet* becomes the first jet airliner to carry passengers.	Boeing begins to develop the idea of a large, wide-bodied jet.	The Boeing 747 makes its first flight.	A jumbo jet is used to test the space shuttle.	A jumbo jet becomes the official plane of the president of the United States.

Timeline

50,000 B.C.E.	The first known boats—dugout canoes, powered by paddles—are used.
10,000 B.C.E.	The first log bridges are used.
4000 B.C.E.	Paved streets may have been used in the city of Ur.
3500 B.C.E.	The wheel is invented in Mesopotamia and Sumeria.
3100 B.C.E.	The first sails are used on boats on the Nile River.
2000 B.C.E.	Horses are first harnessed to wheeled vehicles.
1500 B.C.E.	The oar is invented. It is three times more efficient than the paddle.
400 B.C.E.	Pillar and beam bridges are used in the Middle East.
300 B.C.E.	The Romans invent *pozzolana,* a waterproof cement.
1620	Cornelius van Drebel's oar-powered submarine makes its first voyage.
1709	Father Bartolomeu de Gusmão demonstrates the idea of the hot air balloon to the Portuguese court.
1783	The Montgolfier brothers invent the first manned air balloon. Jacques Charles invents the hydrogen balloon. Marquis Joffroy d'Abbans makes the first voyage in a steam-powered boat, *Peryscaphe.*
1804	Richard Trevithick runs a steam locomotive on a rail line in Wales. Sir George Cayley makes the first successful **glider.**
1807	Robert Fulton introduces the first steamship passenger service, which runs between New York City and Albany.
1816	John Loudon McAdam develops a method of building a three-layer road.
1817	The first bicycle, the draisienne, is introduced.
1825	George Stephenson builds the first public railroad line, from Stockton to Darlington, England.
1841	The invention of woven iron cable makes possible the development of modern **suspension** bridges.
1859	Étienne Lenoir invents the **internal combustion engine.**
1863	The Metropolitan Line, the world's first underground rail service, opens in London.
1869	The first steam-powered motorcycle is introduced.

1879	Werner von Siemens unveils an electric-powered train at the Berlin Exhibition.
1884	Charles Parsons invents the **steam turbine.**
1885	John K. Starley's Rover Safety bicycle is the first modern-style bicycle.
	Gottlieb Daimler produces the first gasoline-engine motorcycle.
	Karl Benz produces the first gasoline-driven internal combustion engine. This invention increases the demand for gasoline.
1886	Karl Benz **patents** the first gasoline-driven car.
	Gottlieb Daimler and Wilhelm Maybach produce the first four-wheeled gasoline-driven car.
	The first oil tanker is built.
1888	John Dunlop invents the **pneumatic tire.**
1890	The City and South London line—the first underground line to use electric trains—is opened.
1903	The Wright brothers make the first airplane flight.
1909	Henry Ford invents the production line to mass-produce cars.
1930	Frank Whittle patents the turbojet engine.
1936	Professor Heinriche Focke's *Focke-Achgelis FA-61,* an early helicopter, makes its first flight.
1939	The *Heinkel He-178,* the world's first jet aircraft, takes to the sky.
	Igor Sikorsky makes the first flight in the *VS-300,* the first single-rotor helicopter.
1955	After building a working model the previous year, Christopher Cockerell patents his hovercraft design.
1956	The first supertankers are built following the closure of the Suez Canal.
1959	The first full-size hovercraft is built. Cockerell pilots it across the English Channel.
1969	The Boeing 747 makes its first flight.
1999	A balloon flies nonstop all the way around the world.

Glossary

Allied belonging to the nations that fought against Germany in World War I and World War II

alloy material made of a metal combined with another metal or other substance

apprentice someone who is learning a trade

axle pole on which a wheel revolves

boiler container for boiling liquid, usually water

cargo goods carried by a ship or other form of transportation

Celt member of an early people that lived mainly in Britain and Ireland

cavalry soldiers on horseback

coffer dam waterproof box built on a river bottom, to allow the building of foundations for a bridge

combat aircraft aircraft carrying weapons

combustion act of burning

commuter person who travels into a city to work

condenser device that filters and compresses a substance, such as steam

congestion overcrowding; often used to describe roads with too many cars on them

crankshaft revolving shaft in an engine, driven by pistons

diesel type of engine that uses compressed air to ignite fuel

domesticate to make tame enough for humans to keep without danger to themselves

empire collection of territories controlled by another country

flammable easily catching fire

friction force in contact with a moving object that slows it down

glider flying machine that does not use an engine

hull main body of a boat

Industrial Revolution period from about 1750 to 1850, when many people moved from the countryside to work in factories and live in cities

internal combustion engine device that uses a fuel such as burning gas mixed with air to power a machine

irrigate to supply land with water through artificial means

isthmus narrow strip of land, mostly surrounded by the sea, that links two larger areas of land

keel part of a boat's frame onto which other parts of the hull are attached

mechanism moving parts in a machine

meteorologist scientist who studies the weather

military having to do with the armed forces

network collection of things that are linked, such as roads and railroads

nuclear power power that makes use of the energy inside atoms

patent official document confirming ownership of a particular invention

periscope device containing mirrors inside a hollow tube that lets the user see what is above him

piston cylinder in an engine that moves up and down to power the crankshaft

pivot small shaft or pin that supports something that turns, such as an oar on the side of a boat

pneumatic tire rubber tire filled with high-pressure air that provides a smooth, comfortable ride

propeller device used by boats or aircraft, with blades connected to a central hub. When turned in water or air, a propeller drives a vehicle along.

propulsion action or process of moving something along

prototype first version of a particular device

radar high-frequency radio waves used to detect the position of distant objects, such as ships and aircraft

refinery factory where a raw material, such as crude oil, is changed into other useful materials, such as gasoline

sprung fitted with springs to reduce jolts caused by impact

steam turbine form of steam engine that uses high-pressure steam to turn a wheel-like device with many blades

stern back of a boat

supersonic flying faster than sound

suspension mechanism that connects the wheels of a vehicle to the rest of it; or the state of hanging from something

technology applying of scientific knowledge in practical ways, using methods and machines made by inventors to make people's lives better

thresh to remove grain from the husks and straw

torpedo self-propelled tubelike weapon, containing explosives, that is launched from a submarine

treadle lever device that is pressed by the foot to drive a machine

turnpike barrier set across a road, that can be passed only after a fee has been paid

twist-grip throttle hand-operated device on a motorcycle that enables the rider to accelerate by turning it

typhoid fever serious contagious disease with symptoms that include fever, diarrhea, and headache

More Books to Read

Erlbach, Arlene. *The Kids' Invention Book.* Minneapolis: The Lerner Publishing Group, 1998.

Kalman, Bobbie and Calder, Kate. *Travel in the Early Days.* New York: Crabtree Publishing Company, 2000.

Tesar, Jenny E. and Bunch, Bryan H. *The Blackbirch Encyclopedia of Science & Invention.* Woodbridge, Conn.: Blackbirch Press, 2001.

Index

airplanes 5, 30, 32–35, 42–43
airships 21
aqueducts 7

balloons 20–21
Benz, Karl 5, 30
bicycles 9, 24–25
bridges 4, 6–7

cargo 4, 13, 40–41, 43
cars 30–31
chariots 4, 11, 14
Cockerell, Christopher 38–39
coffer dam 7

Daimler, Gottlieb 28, 30
diesel engines 16, 17, 23, 31
domesticated animals 4, 6, 14, 15

electrical engines 16, 17
electric trains 23, 27

Ford, Henry 30–31

gasoline engines 5, 28, 30, 33
gliders 32, 33

helicopters 5, 30, 36–37
highways 9

horses 4, 14–15
hovercraft 38–39

Industrial Revolution 11, 15
internal combustion engine 5, 15, 30, 36, 38, 40

jet aircraft 5, 34–35, 42–43
jet engines 5, 34–35, 42
jumbo jets 42–43

lateen sails 13
locomotives 5, 22–23, 26, 27

Montgolfier brothers 20–21
mopeds 29
motorcycles 28–29, 30

nuclear power 17, 19

pillar and beam bridges 6, 7
pneumatic tires 11, 25
pontoon bridges 6
propellers 13, 16, 18, 33, 34, 36, 39

roads 8–9
rollers 10

Roman bridges 7
Roman roads 8

saddles 14
sailing ships 12–13
scooters 29
sledges 10
stagecoaches 15
steam engines 5, 18, 22, 28
steam power 5, 13, 15, 18–19, 22–23, 26, 28, 30, 32
steamships 18–19
steam turbines 19
Stephenson, George 23
stirrups 14
submarines 16–17
subways 26–27
supertankers 4, 40–41
suspension bridges 6, 7

traffic congestion 25, 26, 29
tricycles 28
tunneling 26
turnpikes 9

waterwheels 11
wheels 4, 10–11
Whittle, Frank 34–35
Wright brothers 32–33